CW01335460

ASK
CAROLINE 1

Caroline Pover
translation by Satomi Matsumaru

2010
Alexandra Press
Tokyo, Japan

Ask Caroline 1 (teacher's edition)

Author: Caroline Pover
Translator: Satomi Matsumaru
Cover design: Christopher May
Inside layout: Christopher May and Caroline Pover with Satomi Matsumaru, Yuriko Miyazaki, and Sannah Nozoe
Proofreaders: Cindy Fujimoto, Shigemasa Fujimoto, and Jessica Ocheltree
Publishing assistant: Chrystel Marincich
Photography: David Stetson http://www.davidstetson.com

Copyright ©2010 by Caroline Pover. Printed on recycled paper. Printed and bound in Japan by Sokosha Printing. All rights reserved. No part of this book may be reproduced in any form or by any electronic or mechanical means, including information storage and retrieval systems, without permission in writing from the publisher, except by a reviewer who may quote brief passages in a review. For information, please contact Alexandra Press via the Ask Caroline website at http://www.askcaroline.com, the author directly at caroline@carolinepover.com (English), or the translator directly at satomi@carolinepover.com (Japanese).

First edition.
First printing.

ISBN 978-4-9900791-9-2
EAN 9784990079192

Although the author and publisher have made every effort to ensure the accuracy and completeness of the information contained in this book, they assume no responsibility for errors, inaccuracies, omissions, or any other inconsistency herein. Caroline Pover and Alexandra Press shall not be liable in the event of incidental or consequential damages in connection with the use of information contained in this book. This applies especially to those who attempt to attach a sanitary pad to a G-string.

For Wendy

CONTENTS

Acknowledgments vii

Preface ix

Translator's Foreword xi

Introduction xiii

Ask Caroline

    why Japan 1

    about kimono 9

    about home life 17

    about friendship 25

    about dating 33

    about sex 41

    about underwear 49

    about careers 57

    about motherhood 65

    about beauty 73

ACKNOWLEDGMENTS

It's said that it is a woman's prerogative to change her mind, and my goodness did I change my mind about the design and layout of this book! So first I'd like to thank the team of people who put up with me exercising that right over and over again! Satomi Matsumaru, Yuriko Miyazaki, and Sannah Nozoe—you were so patient with me as we met again and again to discuss the look and feel of this whole project, only to have me then change my mind about everything and do something completely different! But Sannah, those cute icons you came up with were always perfect.

Thanks also to Chris May, a man who truly understands what women want and was able to make sense of what this particular woman wanted and come up with a cover that everyone fell in love with! In fact, both of the designs you came up with were so great that we held a survey to let Japanese women choose their favourite for the Japanese edition—so I also thank those 100 women who took the time to vote!

Thank you to two other men who were part of this project, Barry Guerin and David Stetson. Barry, it was always so much fun for Satomi and me to get together with you and talk about the website. David, I have been such a fan of your photography for so long now that I thought there wasn't any way you could impress me even more than you already had ... and then you shot the photo for the cover for this book and its Japanese companion edition. Thank you so much. And on the subject of cover photos, I am very grateful to the wonderful women who posed for the cover of this teacher's edition—Chika, Chrystel, Kyoko, Masami, Momo, Sumiko, Taeko, and Victoria—you are all beautiful, inside and out!

I thank Cindy and Shigema Fujimoto for their proofreading and for the pleasure of working with them on yet another project. I thank you also to Jessica Ocheltree for her proofreading. And a big thank you to my publishing assistant Chrystel Marincich, who has to be one of the quickest, most efficient people I have ever worked with!

Yuriko, it has been such fun working with you again. Your input on all aspects of the book was invaluable and I appreciate how you managed to squeeze in time with Satomi and me when you have such a hectic schedule! And Satomi, when I first wrote this book several years ago, I always had you in my mind and heart as the perfect translator to work with. Thank you so much for your sensitivity and the understanding of me that you have, which enables you to convey my words to others in a language that I shamefully still have not mastered. The whole experience of working on this book with you has been such a joy, and I am looking forward to working on more projects together!

And a big thank you to my husband, who I don't think has actually read any of my other books, but was consumed by this one as I was writing it, along with the material for the rest of the series. You've always been so excited about this series and haven't minded at all when I've shared some very private thoughts and experiences, sometimes about our life together, sometimes about old boyfriends, and sometimes about my single days. That takes a very secure partner, which has always been one of the things I love about you.

And finally, a very big thank you to all the Japanese women who submitted questions for this series. Needless to say, you shall remain nameless! But I'm very grateful to all of you, along with the many Japanese women I have taught, worked with, employed, given speeches to, and got drunk with! The questions you unabashedly asked me about the lives and loves (and yes, the boobs and bums!) of foreign women are now answered.

Caroline Pover

PREFACE

When I came to Japan as a teacher in 1996 I was lucky enough to meet a wonderful Japanese woman who became my first private language student. A diligent teacher, I always carefully prepared for our lessons, but soon came to realize that my student's priority wasn't really improving her grammar. What she actually wanted was to connect with a foreign woman and learn about her background, culture, opinions, experiences, and perspectives on life. My student had dreams of moving to England some day, so she was particularly interested in connecting with a British woman, which is why she had chosen me as her teacher.

Six months later I was hired as a teacher at an alternative international Japanese high school, where the students happened to be predominantly female. "Language Lab" classes somehow always turned into discussions more akin to those that occur between an auntie and a special niece, or perhaps a big sister and a younger one. The girls talked openly about many aspects of their personal lives and shared their worries about life as a woman. (As for the odd boy or two in those classes, I have often wondered whether the experience either made them wonderful future partners or put them off women for life!) My students said they felt they could talk about things with me that they couldn't with any of the other adults in their lives, and that they didn't feel very comfortable talking about such things in their native language—speaking about them in English felt more natural.

I know I'm not the only foreign woman who has experienced this connection with her female language students.

As my life moved on from that of a teacher to one of a writer, publisher, and speaker, the Japanese women close to me were no longer students; they became readers, employees, and business associates. When I founded *Being A Broad* magazine in 1997, and released my first book, *Being A Broad in Japan: Everything a Western woman needs to survive and thrive*, in 2001, I was amazed to find that both the magazine and the book were so popular with Japanese women—the book was even featured on Japanese television! I learned that when Japanese women who had spent some time living overseas returned to Japan, they felt quite similar to the way foreign women in Japan felt, and found that the topics discussed in my publications resonated with them, too.

I was asked to write a column for the *Weekly Student Times*, published by *The Japan Times*. The editor wanted me just to write about my experiences and opinions as an international woman living in Japan, and I found that I loved writing this column! I received letters from people all over Japan, but especially from women, telling me how much they enjoyed reading my work. One lady in Chiba wrote me the sweetest letter saying how much my articles encouraged her to study English and also to enjoy her own country more. She said my writing had a "happy twinkle," which really touched my heart—I still keep her letter on my desk!

I've had several Japanese female employees over the years and, as is often the case with people I work with, those relationships sometimes moved into friendships. Because a lot of my work in Japan has been related to providing support for international women living here, many of the people who apply to work with me tend to be interested in women's lives. So we would often find ourselves talking about all sorts of issues related to being women—careers, relationships, and self-confidence were frequent topics of conversation—but we had the added element of learning about the cultural backgrounds that our decisions and opinions were steeped in. Because I was a little older than my staff and always willing to be a shoulder to cry on, they started secretly calling me "Nee-san," which is used to refer to someone who is a bit like a big sister to you. When I later found out about their nickname for me, I was actually quite honoured, and I use it today as my Japanese Twitter name (CaroNeeSan).

Throughout my time in Japan, my students, employees, friends, and business associates have asked me so many questions purely because I am a foreign woman—not out of superficial curiosity about foreign culture, but out of a genuine desire to learn from another woman's experiences in order to further develop their own perspectives. Some of those questions were serious and about careers or work–life balance, some of them were sad and about difficulties in relationships or confidence levels, and some of them were really saucy and about waxing our pubic hair or oral sex! I collected those questions and decided to simply answer them, just as if we were having a chat over a coffee.

I hope this series gives you, as a teacher, something fun yet educational to share with your female students. I can tell you that, through discussing all these topics over the years, I've learnt just as much about Japanese women's backgrounds, culture, opinions, experiences, and perspectives on life as they may have done about ours.

TRANSLATOR'S FOREWORD

I first met Caroline in 2002 when she was working on a project called Go Girls, which provided a safe, fun, and supportive English learning environment for women in Japan. But Go Girls wasn't just about studying English; Caroline wanted to provide an opportunity for women to empower other women, through cross-cultural communication.

Four years later, Caroline became seriously ill and spent some time battling a critical health condition. But she came back to us with this series of books; an even more empowering tool to inspire Japanese women looking to expand their world by learning from the perspectives and experiences of women from other cultures and countries.

If I had to describe Caroline in one sentence, I would say "She is one hell of a woman!" This is not because she suffered three strokes when she was only in her early thirties, yet remains "genki," nor because she is relentlessly active and optimistic in a country that is still quite closed to foreign things and people. I describe her as I do because she is simply extraordinarily tough and full of energy and ideas! I believe her strength comes from her strong desire to connect with people, and her willingness to share what she has to offer to society here in Japan.

There are more and more opportunities for us to communicate with non-Japanese people as we are moving into this "global era." But being able to conduct conversations in English doesn't necessarily make us "international." We need to understand the cultures and the backgrounds of the people with whom we communicate in order to have a meaningful connection.

I am a translator and interpreter, and people always assume that I spent my childhood abroad or was exposed to English environments. However, it wasn't until I was an adult that I actually started learning English properly. Acquiring this particular language wasn't "study" for me at all, as I love the language and the challenges that come with it. I believe that learning has to be fun, and the *Ask Caroline* series gives readers just that—a fun way to learn a language, as well as the culture of the people who use it. I love the idea of empowering women, which is Caroline's lifework. I've always been fascinated by this particular aspect of her work and I am glad to find myself working with her again!

I hope that readers of this book will enjoy learning new phrases and expressions in English while coming to understand the experiences of foreign people in Japan—may this lead to meaningful and profound communication that is beyond language abilities. And I also hope that you enjoy catching a glimpse of Caroline's positive attitude toward life, which we can all benefit from and apply in our own lives.

Satomi Matsumaru

INTRODUCTION

This book is for every female language teacher who has been totally and utterly bored by the resources available for use in lessons with their Japanese women students. As anyone who has ever been a private language teacher in Japan knows, most students simply want to talk, and most female students with female teachers want to talk about the girly stuff. Even if you're not a language teacher, you will have discovered that many of your Japanese colleagues, neighbours, and friends want to talk about the girly stuff, are curious about the similarities and differences in being a woman from the Japanese culture and being one from a non-Japanese culture, and have a tendency to ask you what we might consider to be inappropriate questions. This book is for you, too.

Women who are studying Japanese might also find this book to be just a little more entertaining than other resources!

This edition is a companion to the first in a series of books aimed at entertaining, educating, and inspiring Japanese women by sharing with them the experiences of women from around the world. Inside these pages you will find answers to questions you may have had posed to you, but never wanted to answer—I've answered them for you.

This book is made up of ten sections, each based on one simple question. They are real questions, posed by real Japanese women, whom I encouraged to ask me any question they had always wanted to ask a foreign woman—there were no taboo topics at all (and later in the series you will see evidence that there really *were not* any taboo topics!). I then answered the questions from the perspective of an "average" Western woman, while asking readers to bear in mind that all foreign women are different, and that not all Western women would have the same opinion or experience. I then shared my personal experience related to that topic in the "Caroline's Story" part of each section.

For this first edition, Satomi, Yuriko, and I chose to include some fairly tame questions—Japanese women inevitably ask why foreign women come to Japan and what we think about different aspects of Japanese culture. They also ask about the relationships that are important to foreign women and give some interesting insights into their own culture in doing so. You'll be surprised at their interest in the kind of underwear many of us wear! And you'll also read about career and lifestyle dilemmas that seem to be common to all women today, irrespective of cultural backgrounds.

If you're using this as a learning tool, don't worry if your students have a low level of English. Everything is written in both English and Japanese, so you can flick back and forth between languages as you go along. The translation has been written with the intention of retaining my original nuance as much as possible, as opposed to being written in more general Japanese, which would mean much of my intent would have been lost. This is intended to be more enjoyable to those reading in both languages.

There are some useful phrases and sentences, with examples of how to use them, and plenty of cultural explanations throughout. There are also a few hints on things that Japanese women should (or shouldn't!) do that will help them to be "women of the world," which is often a concern of theirs before they travel overseas. And finally, there are some questions that might inspire some open-ended discussions between you and your students or friends. And don't forget that there is an edition just for Japanese women, if your students are keen to have their own copies.

You can use this book in any way you like! You don't have to start from the beginning and read it in order ... you can dip in and out of the book as you feel like it. If you're keen to use this as a learning tool, I recommend encouraging your students to read all the useful phrases first, and then have them try to read the English sections on what average foreign women think, and then my own story. After they've done that, try out some of the Talking Points in class. And don't forget that the audio CD will help your students listen to the book being read in a British accent (yes, it's really me!), and perhaps save some of your blushes at having to read elements of the book out loud in class!

And if you're reading this because you think it will be a fun thing to share with your Japanese girlfriends, why not sit around with a bottle of wine, giggling about some of the predicaments we women find ourselves in?!

ASK
CAROLINE
... WHY JAPAN

キャロライン姉さんに質問！
どうして日本なの？

employer ... 雇用主 specific to ... 〜に特有の martial art ... 武道 the pay ... 報酬、支払い、給与 fascinated by ... 〜に魅了される、〜に心を奪われる to spark their interest ... 興味を掻き立てられる independently ... 自力で、単独で、自立して to refer to as ... 〜と呼ばれる、〜とみなされる significant ... 著しい restless ... 落ち着きのない、せかせかした primary school teacher ... 小学校の先生 to suggest ... 提案する qualifications ... 資格 to be honest ... 正直なところ limited ... 限られた、わずかな naïve ... ウブ to turn up and see ... そこに行って様子を見てみる

どうして日本なの？

> どうして日本に来たのですか？
> 外国の人たちはどうしてこの国に
> 興味を持っているの？

来日する人たちの中には、会社の都合で家族と一緒に日本に来る人もいるし、語学や、例えば武道など特定の科目を勉強するための留学目的で来る人もいます。それから日本ではお給料がとてもいいので、英語を教えるために来日する人もいます。単に冒険を求めて来日する人だっています！多くの外国人にとって、日本ってとても興味深い国なんです。なぜなら、言葉や文化が西洋の国々のそれとはまったく違うから。中には、日本にまつわる本を読んだり、映画を観たり、誰かから話を聞いて興味をそそられて、子供の頃から日本に夢中だったっていう人もいます。

自力で日本に来た外国人の中には、「expats」と呼ばれるのを嫌がる人もいます。なぜなら「expats」という言葉は、日本に来る際に莫大な金銭的・心理的な支えが与えられることを示唆する一方で、自力で来日する人たちはたいていの場合、何の手助けもないからです。

WHY JAPAN?

Why did you come to Japan? Why are foreigners interested in this country?

Some people are sent here by their employer and their family comes with them; some come to study Japanese or to study something specific to Japan, such as a martial art; some come because they want to teach English and the pay is quite good in Japan; some come just to have an adventure! Japan is an interesting country to many foreigners because the language and culture are so different to those of Western countries. Some people become fascinated by Japan when they are children; maybe they read a book, watched a movie, or heard some stories about Japan, and this sparked their interest.

Some foreigners who came to Japan independently don't like to be referred to as "expats" because the word implies a significant amount of financial and emotional support when moving to Japan; people who came to Japan independently usually had to deal with the move without any help.

どうして日本なの?

キャロラインの場合

私は、冒険を求めて日本に来ました！英国にいた頃、私は割と落ち着きのない小学校の先生でした。仕事は大好きだったけど、どこかに、もっと何かがあるんじゃないかと思っていました。それが何であるかは分からなかったけど。15ヶ月ほど日本に住んだ友達がいたのですが、彼女が日本で英語を教えたらって勧めてくれました。私が教員免許を持っているので、教師としていい仕事が見つかるはずだと言っていました。正直なところ、それ以前は日本に来るなんて考えたこともありませんでした。小さい頃からアジア文化のとりこになっているタイプじゃなかったから。実際のところ、日本に関しての知識なんてほとんどなかったし、すごくウブだったと思います。もちろん、日本語をまったくしゃべれなかったし。

でも、日本に引っ越すって考えに心のどこかでとってもワクワクしている自分がいました！イングランドからこれほど遠い所で、まったく違う文化、違う言語の中で過ごすということが、とても魅力的で、私にとってすごくワクワクすることだったんです！それから、来日前に仕事を見つけることはしたくありませんでした——ただ日本に到着して、どうなるか様子を見たかったんです！私にとっては、すべてが冒険の一部だったから！

WHY JAPAN?

Caroline's Story

I came to Japan for an adventure! I was a rather restless primary school teacher in the UK. I loved my job, yet I knew there was something more for me somewhere—I just didn't know what it was. A friend of mine had spent about 15 months in Japan and she suggested that I go to Japan to teach English. She said that, because of my education qualifications, I would be able to get a very good job in teaching. To be honest, I had never thought about coming to Japan before—I wasn't one of those people who had been fascinated by Asian culture their whole lives—in fact, my knowledge of Japan was extremely limited and I am sure I was very naïve. I certainly didn't speak any of the language.

But something in me got so excited about the idea of moving to Japan! I loved the idea of it being so far away from England, being such a completely different culture, and having such a completely different language. That all sounded very exciting to me! And I didn't want to find a job before coming—I just wanted to turn up and see what happened. To me, that was all part of the adventure!

どうして日本なの？

relocation（転勤、移住） Usually refers to a situation where someone was sent to Japan by their employer. 通常は、会社の都合で日本に転勤する場合などに使用します。

- "I was relocated to Japan"
  「日本に転勤してきました」

- "A relocation company helped us move here"
  「リロケーション会社が日本への引越しを手伝ってくれました」

- "I'd like to relocate next year"
  「来年転勤したいな」

local hire（現地採用） Used to refer to foreigners who are not on expat packages but are working in a profession other than English teaching. 駐在員として日本にいるのではなく、また、英語を教える仕事に就いているわけでもない人を指します。

- "She is a local hire"
  「彼女は現地採用よ」

- "She is on a local hire package"
  「彼女は現地採用待遇です」

WHY JAPAN?

to move overseas（海外に引っ越す）Can be used for any situation. どの場合でも使えます。

- "She moved overseas last year"
  「彼女は去年、海外に引っ越しました」

- "I'd like to move overseas when I retire"
  「仕事を辞めたら海外に引っ越したいな」

- "Why did you move overseas?"
  「どうして海外に引っ越したのですか?」

expatriate（駐在員）Short version: expat; technically means anybody living out of their home country, but foreigners in Japan tend to use it to refer to people who are sent by their companies and compensated well for it—"expat package." 短縮形：expat；正確には、自国以外に暮らす人を指す言葉ですが、現実には、日本に住む外国人は、会社の都合により転勤して来て、その代わりに非常にいい条件『駐在員待遇』を受けている人たちのことを指す場合が多いです。

- "They are on an expat package"
  「彼らは駐在員待遇で来日しているのよ」

- "Tokyo American Club has a lot of expatriate members"
  「東京アメリカンクラブには多くの駐在員会員がいます」

- "I didn't come to Japan as an expat"
  「駐在員として来日したのではありません」

どうして日本なの？

TALKING POINTS
トーキング・ポイント

- Have you ever lived overseas? What was it like?
  海外に住んだことはありますか？どんな感じでしたか？

- Would you like to live overseas? If so, why? If not, why not?
  海外に住んでみたいですか？住んでみたい場合、それはどうしてですか？住みたくない場合、それはどうしてですか？

- What countries would you like to live in?
  どの国に住んでみたいですか？

- Which countries do you think would be the best for a woman to relocate to and why?
  女性が引っ越す先として一番いい国はどこだと思いますか？それは何故ですか？

- How would you feel if you moved overseas as an independent woman?
  自立した女性として海外に引っ越すとしたらどう感じると思いますか？

- How about if you moved because of your partner's job?
  もしあなたが配偶者の仕事の都合で引っ越すとしたらどう感じるでしょうか？

Did you know?

The number of foreigners that entered Japan in 2009 was around 9 million (including tourists).
2009年に日本に入国した外国人数は約900万人でした（観光客を含む）。

ASK
CAROLINE
... ABOUT KIMONO

キャロライン姉さんに質問！
着物について。

to cater to ... ～に（サービスなどを）提供する to manage to ... ～を何とかやり遂げる curves ... カーブ（身体の線など） niece ... 姪 funky ... ファンキー、かっこいい trainers ... 運動靴 self-conscious ... 照れくさい to pay attention to ... ～に気を付ける、注意する to spend ages doing ... 長い時間をかけて～する wig ... カツラ to transform into ... ～に変身する tomboy ... おてんば

着物について

着物を着てみたいと思いますか？

日本に住んでいる西洋人女性はたいてい、着物を着てみたいと思っていますよ。観光客向けの場所もいくつかあり、外国人向けに着物試着の広告を出しています。私たちが自分で着物を着るなんて到底ムリですから、誰かに手伝ってもらう必要があります。外国人女性の多くは、浴衣を着る方がよっぽど簡単だと感じていて、花火やお祭りに行く際に浴衣を着たりもします。でも、日本人女性が着るのと同じようにはまったくなりません。なぜなら私たち西洋人女性は、豊満な体型である人が多い一方、着物は昔から、比較的まっすぐな体型の女性向けに作られているからです。

あなたの外国人の女友達は恐らく浴衣とか着物をどうやって着るのか知らないので、手伝うよって言えばきっと喜んでくれますよ！

KIMONO

Do you want to try wearing a kimono?

Most Western women living in Japan like to try dressing up in a kimono. There are several places that cater to tourists and advertise for foreigners to come and try one on. We can't possibly manage to put on a kimono by ourselves, so we need someone to help us do it. Many foreign women find putting on yukata much easier and often wear them in summer to watch fireworks or go to festivals. They never quite look the same on us as they do on Japanese women though, because we usually have a lot of curves and kimonos are traditionally made for women with straighter bodies.

Your foreign girlfriend probably doesn't know how to put on a yukata or a kimono and would really appreciate your offer to help!

着物について

キャロラインの場合

一番上の姪っ子が12歳の時に私に会いに日本に来た際、私がその子を連れて行ったところの一つに、着物の試着がありました。彼女はいつもジーンズにファンキーなTシャツと運動靴というように、とってもカジュアルな服装をしている若い女の子なので、着物を着てみるという考えは少し照れくさかったけれど、実はこっそり楽しみにしていたのでした。

着物屋さんの女性店員たちは、姪っ子にとても気を使ってくれました。着物用の肌着を着せた後に姪っ子を座らせ、舞妓さんのようなメイクをものすごい時間をかけて施してくれました。顔にはあの真っ白で独特なメイク、赤いアイシャドウ、黒いアイライナーを入れてもらい、真っ赤な口紅を独特な形に塗ってもらいました。そんなメイクの中、姪っ子の青い瞳はとっても異様でした！その後さらに肌着を着せて、その上から着物を着せました。姪っ子は自分が気に入った伝統的なカツラを選び、下駄を履きました。建物を出て日本庭園に入り、着物の袖を腕にまわし、下駄を履いた足で小またに歩いていました。私の姪っ子は、ちっちゃなおてんば娘から、非常に洗練された感じの若い女性に大変身を遂げたのです。彼女は、とっても気に入っていました！

KIMONO

Caroline's Story

My eldest niece came to visit me in Japan when she was twelve, and one of the things I took her to do was try on a kimono. She is usually quite a casually dressed young woman and wears jeans, funky t-shirts and trainers most of the time. She was a little bit self-conscious about the idea of trying on a kimono, but was secretly quite looking forward to it.

The ladies in the kimono shop paid a great deal of attention to my niece. They put on special undergarments, then sat her down and spent ages doing her make-up so that she looked like a maiko. She had the special white make-up put on her face, then the red eyeshadow, black eyeliner, and red lips painted into a special shape. Her blue eyes looked very strange with that make-up! Then they put on more layers of undergarments and then the kimono itself. She chose a traditional wig that she liked and put on geta. She walked out of the building and into the Japanese garden, holding the sleeves of her kimono over her arm and taking little steps in her geta. My niece had been transformed from a little tomboy into a very elegant-looking young woman. And she loved it!

着物について

to try on（試着する）To put on an item of clothing to see how it looks. 似合うかどうか服を試着すること。

- "I'd like to try on that dress"
  「あのドレスを試着してみたいわ」

- "Where can I try this on?"
  「試着はどこでできますか？」

- "What a nice suit! You should try that on"
  「素敵なスーツ！試着してみるべきよ」

to dress up（ドレスアップする、おしゃれする）To wear clothing for a special purpose; sometimes a special costume. 特別な目的のための洋服を着ること。特別な衣装の場合も。

- "We're going to dress up for the party tonight"
  「今夜のパーティ用におしゃれするわよ」

- "I went to a Halloween party dressed up as a witch"
  「魔女の格好をしてハロウィーン・パーティに出たの」

- "I have to dress up for my friend's wedding. Can you help me?"
  「友達の結婚式用にドレスアップしなきゃ。手伝ってくれる？」

fit（合う、ピッタリ）
The way that clothes match your size (can be a noun or a verb). 洋服がサイズに合っていること（動詞としても名詞としても使えます）。

- "That dress is a perfect fit"
  「そのドレス、ちょうどピッタリね」

- "That suit fits you perfectly"
  「そのスーツすごくピッタリね」

- "That doesn't quite fit you properly. How about trying this one?"
  「あなたにちゃんと合ってないみたい。こっちを試してみたら？」

complimenting other women（他の女性を褒める）

- "That really suits you!"
  「それすごく似合ってるわ！」

- "That colour looks great on you!"
  「その色、あなたにすごく似合うわ！」

- "You really know how to dress up!"
  「おしゃれの仕方をよく知っているのね！」

- "I really love your style"
  「あなたの格好、素敵だわ」

着物について

TALKING POINTS
トーキング・ポイント

- In what kinds of situations do you like to wear kimono?
  どのような時に着物を着たいですか？

- How do you find wearing a kimono? Is it comfortable?
  着物を着るのってどんな感じですか？着心地はいいですか？

- What happened the first time you tried wearing a kimono?
  着物を初めて着たとき、どんなことがありましたか？

- What are your favourite national costumes and why?
  好きな民族衣装は何ですか？それはなぜですか？

- Have you tried on any other country's national costume?
  他の国の民族衣装を着てみたことはありますか？

- Do you know of any national costumes that are very easy for women to wear?
  女性にとって着易い民族衣装は何か知っていますか？

- How about for the men?
  男性にとって着易いのはどうでしょうか？

Did you know?
The Kyoto community wanted to encourage people to wear kimono, so they gave special passports to suitably attired visitors—this entitled the holders to great discounts at lots of tourist spots!
京都では地域一体となって、着物の着用を促進すべく「京都きものパスポート」を発行していました。着物を着てこれを提示すれば、観光地で割引などが受けられました！

ASK
CAROLINE
... ABOUT HOME LIFE

キャロライン姉さんに質問！
家について。

adulthood ... 成人期　considered to be ... 〜と思われる　to admit ... 認める　lack of ability ... 能力の欠如　dependence ... 依存、頼りにすること　excuse ... 言い訳　fib ... ウソ　to worry about ... 〜を心配する　to reassure ... 〜を安心させる　to explore ... 探索する　occupied by ... 〜が占める、〜に占領される　transition ... 移行

家について

**西洋人女性は、大人に
なっても親と一緒に住んでいる
日本人男性・女性のことを本当は
どう思っているの？**

西洋人女性のほとんどは、大人になっても親と一緒に住むことについて、とても奇妙だと感じると思います。親と一緒に住んでいることを認めるのは、非常に恥ずかしいことだと考えられています。なぜなら、親と一緒に住むということは、自分自身の生活を作る能力に欠けるということや、金銭的・精神的に親に依存していることになるからです。でも、日本は違います。住む場所を見つけ親から離れるのはとても高くつくからです。多くの日本人は実家近くの大学に行きますが、西洋人のほとんどは、実家を出る格好の理由になるため、実家から遠い場所にある大学に行くものです。

もし両親と一緒に住んでいることを認めたくなければ、「家／マンションを人とシェアしているの」とか、「大家さんが一緒に住んでいます」と言うこともできます。決してウソではないですから！

HOME LIFE

What do Western women really think of Japanese men and women who live at home way into adulthood?

Most Western women would think it was very strange to live with their parents during adulthood. It would be considered to be very embarrassing to admit that you lived with your parents, because it would show a lack of ability to create your own life and a dependence on your parents, financially and emotionally. But Japan is different; it can be very expensive to find your own place and move away from your parents. Many Japanese people go to university near their home town and most Westerners go to university very far away from their home town, which is a great excuse to leave their parents' homes.

If you don't want to admit that you live with your parents, you can always say "I share a house/apartment with others," or "My landlord/lady lives with me"; it's not technically a fib!

家について

キャロラインの場合

私は18歳の時、大学に行くために初めて実家を出ました。自立することをとても楽しみにしていましたが、同時に、母親を1人にしてしまうのが少し心配でした。母親は何度も私に心配ないと言って、家を出て世界を見て来るべきだ、さもなければ自分は母親として失格だと感じてしまう、と言いました。母はいつも私を勇気付けてくれました。

大学には寮が何棟かあり、ほとんどの部屋は1年生が住んでいました。全員個室を持っていて、お風呂、トイレ、ラウンジ、食堂を共同で使っていました。私が住んでいた寮には400人くらいの学生がおり、各階には10部屋くらいありました。とっても大きな寮だったんです！両親と一緒の生活から自立した生活への移行を容易にするため食事はすべて用意されたので、自分で作る心配をする必要はありませんでした。

この寮で、何人かの素晴らしい友人ができました。実家を出た最初の年に、特別なひとときを何度も一緒に過ごし、2年目に全員が寮を出て自分のアパートを見つけた後も、ずっと仲良しの友達であり続けました。今だって一番の仲良しなんですよ！

HOME LIFE

Caroline's Story

I first left home when I was 18 years old, when I moved away to university. I was really looking forward to being independent, but at the same time, I was rather worried about leaving my mum alone. She reassured me many times, telling me that she expected me to leave home and explore the world and that she would feel like a failure as a mother if I didn't. She always encouraged me.

The university had halls of residence, which were mostly occupied by first-year students. Everybody had their own private rooms and we shared bathrooms, toilets, a lounge, and a dining room. There were about 400 students in my halls of residence and there were about ten rooms on each floor. It was a very large place! To ease the transition from living with parents to living independently, all meals were provided so we didn't have to worry about cooking for ourselves.

I made some wonderful friends in those halls of residence. We shared so many special times during our first year away from home, and even when we all moved out of the halls and found our own apartments for our second year, we stayed really close friends. We are still the closest of friends today!

家について

to rent a room（部屋を借りる）You pay the owner for one room within a house or apartment, but use some common facilities; nothing is actually in your name. 家やマンション内にある一部屋分の家賃をオーナーに対して払い、共有部分も使用できるものです。ただし、自分名義なものは一つもないことになります。

- "I'm renting a room from my friend"
  「友達に部屋を借りているの」

to share a flat/apartment/house（マンション／家をシェアする）You rent or own the location together and share all facilities equally; both your names could be on any official documents. 場所を共同で借りたり所有したりして、すべての設備を平等に使うこと。公的な書類には、全員の名前が記載されます。

- "I share a place with my friend"
  「この場所は友達と一緒にシェアしています」

HOME LIFE

curfew（門限） Time you have to be home by. それまでに帰宅しなければいけない時間。

- "My dormitory has a midnight curfew"
「寮の門限は夜の12時です」

- "I gave my teenage daughter a 9pm curfew after I caught her smoking"
「10代の娘がタバコを吸っているのを見つけて以来、門限は夜9時にしています」

- "I can't go on to the next party because I'm on a curfew tonight"
「次のパーティには行けないの、今夜は門限までに帰らなきゃいけないから」

to take/bring someone home（家に人を連れて帰る）

- "I can't bring anyone home ... we will have to stay at your place"
「家には誰も連れて行けないの…あなたの家に泊まるしかないわ」

- "I can't have any overnight guests ... let's go to a love hotel"
「人は泊められないの…ラブ・ホテルに行きましょう」

- "Let me ask my parents if I can take you home"
「あなたを家に連れて来ていいか親に聞いてみるわ」

- "I'm not going home with you ... Maybe another time!"
「あなたの家にはついて行かないわ…また今度ね！」

家について

TALKING POINTS
トーキング・ポイント

- If you still live with your parents, what are the reasons? If you have left home, what were the reasons?
もしあなたがまだ親と住んでいる場合、その理由は何ですか？もし親元を出ている場合、その理由は何でしたか？

- What do you think are the advantages and disadvantages of living with and without your parents?
親と一緒に住むこと、または一緒に住まないことの利点と欠点は何だと思いますか？

- If you had children, at what age would you like them to leave home and why?
もしあなたに子供がいたとしたら、何歳で家を出て欲しいと思いますか？それは何故ですか？

- Do you think it is different if a man lives with his parents or if a woman lives with her parents? If so, how?
男性が親元で暮らすのと、女性が親元で暮らすのとでは違うと思いますか？もし違うとしたら、それはどう違うと思いますか？

- Would you like to live with your parents again during their senior years?
親が年を取ってからまた一緒に住みたいと思いますか？

Did you know?
The average age for young people to leave home in the UK is 21. In Japan it is 27.
英国で子供が実家を出る平均年齢は21歳。日本は27歳。

ASK
CAROLINE
... ABOUT FRIENDSHIP

キャロライン姉さんに質問!
友情について。

a general rule ... 一般的に perspective ... 見方 to miss out on ... 〜を見逃す situation ... 状況 boost your ego ... 自尊心を高める compliment ... 褒め言葉 hug ... ハグ,抱擁 fuss about nothing ... 何でもないことを騒ぎ立てる to hang out ... 時間を過ごす comforted ... 慰められる to adore ... 敬愛する protective ... 保護する curious ... 好奇心を持った mutual friend ... 共通の友達 hilarious ... とても面白い hint ... ほのめかし、ヒント

友情について

一般的に、日本の女性は男性の友達を作りません。でもどうして西洋人女性は男友達がいるの？

男友達は、違った角度から人生の見方を示してくれます。助言を求めて女友達だけと話していたら、その状況に対して違った見方をするかもしれない男性の視点を逃してしまいます。また、例えば恋人はいらないけど男性と一緒にいたいという時、男友達は素晴らしいものです。男友達はたいてい褒め言葉で自尊心をくすぐってくれるけど、その目的がセックスじゃないことは明らかです。そして彼らの温かく力強いハグは絶対必要！彼らは守り、気にかけてくれ、もしあなたが些細なことでクヨクヨしていたら、率直にそう言ってくれるはずです！

恋愛としては興味がないけれど友達でいたい男性と出会った場合、「今は誰ともデートする気はないんだけど、男性と一緒にいるのは楽しいわ。たまには一緒に出かける（hang out）？」と言うのもいいでしょう（『hang out』はカジュアルな表現で、恋愛の間柄には使いません）。

FRIENDSHIP

As a general rule, Japanese women don't have male friends. Why do Western women have male friends?

Male friends bring a different perspective on life. If we only ever talk to female friends for advice, then we miss out on the perspective that men could bring to a situation. Male friends are great if we are choosing not to date at that time in our lives, but still like to have male company. Guy friends often will boost your ego with compliments, and you know they're not after sex. And a warm, strong hug from a male friend is something not to be missed! They're protective and caring, and will tell you directly if you're making a fuss about nothing!

If you meet a man that you would like to be friends with but are not interested in romantically, you can always say "I am taking a break from dating, but do enjoy male company. Would you like to hang out sometime?" ("Hang out" is very casual and not often used in romantic situations.)

友情について

キャロラインの場合

私には、アンドリューというとっても良い友達がいます。2002年以来の友達で、いつも私のそばにいてくれました。私の喜びも悲しみも、ともに分かち合ってきました。彼は私とともに一緒に笑い、私が感情的になった時には慰めてくれました。まるでお兄さんみたいな感じです。彼には、私が敬愛してやまない素晴らしい日本人の奥さんがおり、私は、彼との友情だけでなく、私がアンドリューの奥さんとの間に彼抜きで育んだ友情にも感謝しています。奥さんは働き者で長い時間仕事をしているので、アンドリューと私は夜2人で飲みに行ったりします。

私が出会ったとある男性について(その人は後に私の夫になるのですが)初めてアンドリューに話した時、アンドリューは私の保護者のようになり、リチャードと会いたがりました。共通の友達のバーベキューにみんなで行き、アンドリューとその奥さんに彼氏を紹介しました。アンドリューの可笑しいことったら！何を考えているのか一切顔には出さず、3時間ほどリチャードに次から次へと質問を浴びせました。リチャードはすべてきちんと答え、バーベキューの最後に、アンドリューはリチャードの手を握り「ようこそ、君も家族の一員だ」って言ったのでした。

Caroline's Story

I have an extremely good friend called Andrew; we have been friends since 2002 and he has always been there for me. He has shared my happy times and sad times. He has laughed with me and comforted me when I have been upset. He is like a big brother to me. He has a wonderful Japanese wife whom I adore, and I am not only thankful for my friendship with him, but also for the friendship that has developed between his wife and me, independent of Andrew. His wife works extremely hard and very long hours, and Andrew and I would often go for drinks together in the evenings.

When I first told Andrew about the man I had met—who would later become my husband—Andrew became very protective and very curious to meet Richard. We all went to a mutual friend's barbecue, where I introduced my boyfriend to Andrew and his wife. Andrew was hilarious! He spent about three hours asking Richard one question after another, without showing any hint of what he was really thinking. Richard handled it all extremely well, and at the end of the barbecue, Andrew held out his hand and said, "Welcome to the family."

友情について

boyfriend vs boy friend
ボーイフレンド＝彼氏 vs 男友達

When written, it is easy to see the difference between the two: the first is a special male friend who you have a romantic relationship with, the second is a friend who is a boy (or male). But when spoken, confusion can occur! 書き言葉の場合、両者の違いは明らかです。前者は、恋愛関係にある特別な男性の友達であり、後者は性別が男の友達ということです。でも話し言葉の場合、混乱が起こります！

Here are some words you can use to refer to your male friends without confusing anyone. 誰のことも混乱させることなく男友達を指す言葉は以下の通りです。

guy friend

- "I'm going out with a guy friend tonight"
  「今夜は男友達と出かけるの」

male friend

- "I have a male friend that I'm going out with tomorrow"
  「明日一緒に出かける男友達がいるわ」

FRIENDSHIP

friends with benefits（セフレ） A situation where you have sex with a friend on a regular basis but are not romantically involved with them. 定期的にセックスをする友達だけれど恋愛感情がない相手。「friends with benefits」という言い方は、単なる「セフレ」というより、友情があることが大前提です。英語で「sex friend」といえば日本語の「セフレ」同様、友情がなくセックスだけを目的とした関係を意味します。

- "I think I'm going to ask him if he wants to be friends with benefits!"
  「セフレになりたいか彼に聞いてみようかな！」

- "I don't want a relationship right now, but I'd love to be friends with benefits!"
  「恋人はいらないけど、セフレは欲しいな！」

- "I'm tired of just being friends with benefits ... I think I want more."
  「ただのセフレでいるのに疲れたわ…もっとちゃんとお付き合いしたい」

platonic（プラトニック） Not involving any kind of sexual relationship; purely on a "friends" basis. 純粋に友情だけの関係で、いかなる性的な関係もないこと。

- "Our relationship is purely platonic"
  「私たちは純粋にプラトニックな関係なの」

- "We have a platonic kind of love"
  「私たちの愛情はプラトニックなの」

- "They really care about each other, but I'm sure it's just platonic"
  「彼らはお互いのこと大切に思っているけど、プラトニックな関係だと思うわ」

友情について

TALKING POINTS
トーキング・ポイント

- If you have male friends, how did your relationships develop?
  もしあなたに男友達がいる場合、その友情はどうやって育ちましたか?

- What is the difference between your friendships with the men and women in your life?
  あなたの人生において、男性との友情と女性との友情の違いは何ですか?

- What do you think about having a romantic relationship first, then becoming just friends afterward?
  最初に恋愛関係になり、その後にただの友達になることについてどう思いますか?

- How about the other way round? Friendship first, then romance?
  その逆はどうでしょうか?友情が先で恋愛が後の場合は?

- In what ways do you think men and women have different expectations of friendship? In what ways do we have similar expectations?
  男性と女性の間で、友情に求めることの違いは何だと思いますか?友情に求めることで似ているのは何だと思いますか?

Did you know?
Western brides are starting to involve their male friends in their weddings, with some even having "bridesmen" along with their bridesmaids.
西洋では最近、花嫁が男友達を自分の結婚式に関わらせるようになってきており、中には花嫁の付添人「ブライズメイド」と一緒に「ブライズマン」がいる場合もあります。

ASK CAROLINE
... ABOUT DATING

キャロライン姉さんに質問！
デートについて。

traditionally ... 伝統的に   inviting ... 誘うこと   initiative ... イニシアチブ   equal ... 平等   to insist on ... 強く主張する   my treat ... 私のおごり   offended ... 気分を害される   respectful ... 礼儀正しい   to dominate ... 支配する、独占する   to split ... 分ける   not to mind ... 気にしない

デートについて

デートでお金を払うのは誰？

伝統的に、デートに誘い、デート中に話題を提供し、そしてデート代を払うのは男性でした。でも現在は多くの女性が、男性をデートに誘い、会話を引っ張っていく自信を持っており、金銭的にも自立しているため、デート代を支払うことだってできます！多くの女性が、デート代の半分を払わないと男性が自分たちに対し権力を握ってしまうと感じています。このような女性たちは、デート代を半分支払うこと、または支払うと申し出ることによって、対等に扱ってもらいたいという意思を示すことができると感じています。

もし彼が支払うと言い張った場合、そしてあなたが彼にもう一度会いたいと思うくらい好意を持った場合は、「じゃあ私が次回払うわね」と言いましょう。この言い方がとてもいい理由は2つあります。1つは、彼はあなたを自立した強い女性だと思うこと。もう一つは、あなたがまた彼に会いたいと思っていることを彼に伝えることができることです。

DATING

Who pays on a date?

Traditionally, men were the ones who did the inviting, led the conversation during, and paid for a date. Many women now feel confident enough to take the initiative in asking a man out on a date, in leading the conversation, and are also financially independent so they can afford to pay for the date, too! Many women feel that if they do not pay for half the date, then the man has power over them. By paying, or offering to pay, for half the date, they feel that they are showing that they want to be considered as an equal.

If he insists on paying and you do like him enough to want to see him again, then you can say "My treat next time," which is good for two reasons: he will see you as an independent, strong woman and he will know that you want to see him again.

デートについて

キャロラインの場合

独身だった頃、常に自分も払うと言い張っていました。付き合って間もない彼氏が自分で支払うと決め付けてお勘定の紙をつかんだので、気分を害されたことも何度かありました。恋愛関係になり得る状況で、食事代を払ってもらうという感覚が嫌いだったんです。

私が夫と出会った時、新たな状況となりました！ある意味、彼は伝統的で、高級レストランに私を連れて行くことが好きでした。私にごちそうするということが、彼にとって楽しみの一つだったからです。心地良いわけではなかったけれど、彼がとても大切な人だと悟った私は、代金を払うことに関して自分がどう感じているのか注意深く考えてみました。彼はいつも私に敬意を払ってくれ、会話を独り占めすることなく、ちゃんと私を対等にみてくれていたのは分かっていました。男性がデート代を払うのが嫌だというのは私の問題であり、彼が悪いわけではないことに気づいたんです！

付き合い始めてから、そして結婚してからも、私たちはすべてきちんと折半しています。ただ、彼がいまだに支払うと言い張るロマンチックな食事だけは彼が支払い、私はそれを気にしないことを学びました！

Caroline's Story

When I was single, I always insisted on sharing the bill, and I sometimes got quite offended if a new man grabbed the cheque and assumed that he would pay. I didn't like the feeling of somebody paying for my meal in a potentially romantic situation.

When I first met my husband, I found myself in a new situation! In some ways, he is a little bit traditional and he enjoyed the idea of taking me out to rather expensive restaurants. Part of the enjoyment for him was that he treated me. I wasn't really very comfortable with this, but I sensed that he was someone very special, so I carefully thought about my feelings about paying for things. I knew that he already looked at me as an equal, he was always respectful, and he didn't dominate our conversations, so I realized that my problem with a man paying for a date was my problem and not his!

Since we have been together, and including after our marriage, we have always split everything pretty equally. Except for the romantic dinners, which he still insists on paying for and I have learnt not to mind at all!

デートについて

to take someone out（誰かをデートに連れ出す）

To invite someone on a date. If you are paying, then you are technically the person doing the taking out. (Note: "to take someone out" can also mean to kill someone and is often heard in gangster movies.) 誰かをデートに誘うこと。もしあなたが支払うのなら、理論的にはあなたがデートに連れ出している側の人物ということです！（「to take someone out」は、誰かを殺すという意味もあり、ギャング映画などでよく使われます。）

- "I'd like to take you out sometime"
  「そのうちあなたとデートしたいわ」

- "Would you mind if I took you out sometime?"
  「あなたを近いうちどこかに連れ出したら嫌かしら？」

handling the bill
支払いをする

- "My treat"「私のおごりよ」
- "It's on me"「私が払います」
- "Let's split the bill"「代金を折半にしましょう」
- "Please allow me to pay"「私に払わせて」
- "OK, I'll get it next time"「わかった。じゃあ次は私が払うわね」

DATING

blind date (ブラインド・デート)
A date where you have not seen the person you are going out with—maybe a friend set you up?! あなたがまだ会ったことのない相手とのデート。友達が設定したりとか？！

- "Can I set you up on a blind date with my friend?"
  「私の友達とブラインド・デートしてみない？」

- "My sister has organised a blind date for me next week"
  「妹(姉)が来週のブラインド・デートをアレンジしてくれました」

- "I'm going on a blind date tonight ... I wonder how it will go!"
  「今夜ブラインド・デートに行くの…うまく行くかしら！」

- "I'm not going on a blind date, so stop trying to set me up!"
  「ブラインド・デートなんてしないから、アレンジするのやめてちょうだい！」

- "I'm very happy being single, so I have no need for blind dates"
  「私はシングルでハッピーだから、ブラインド・デートは必要ないわ」

casual dating (気軽なデート)
Not really dating anyone seriously or on a regular or exclusive basis. 真剣に誰かとデートしているわけではなく、定期的に、または1人の相手とだけデートしているわけではない場合。

- "I'm just casually dating a few people at the moment"
  「今は気軽に何人かとデートしているの」

- "We've planned to go on a casual date ... no expectations"
  「気軽なデートに行く予定よ…何も期待せずね」

- "He only wants to go on casual dates and I'm looking for something a bit more right now, so I don't want to waste my time"
  「彼は気軽なデートをしたいだけで、私はそれよりもっと深いものを求めているから、時間を無駄にしたくないわ」

デートについて

TALKING POINTS
トーキング・ポイント

- What is your ideal kind of date?
  あなたにとって理想的なデートとはどんなデートですか?

- Have you taken the lead and asked a man out on a date before? Do you think it affected anything?
  これまで、男性をリードして自分から男性をデートに誘ったことはありますか?そのことが何かに影響したと思いますか?

- How would you like to ask someone out on a date?
  誰かをデートに誘いたいと思いますか?

- In long-term relationships, do you think it is important to still make time for going on dates?
  長くお付き合いしている場合、それでも相手とデートするために時間を作ることは大切なことだと思いますか?

- Have you ever taken a man out on a date and paid for it yourself?
  これまで、男性をデートに誘い、自分がデート代を支払ったことはありますか?

- How would you handle it if you were on a date and decided you didn't like him?
  もしあなたがデート中に、彼のことが好きじゃないことに気づいたら、どう切り抜けますか?

Did you know?
48% of first dates in America end with a kiss.
アメリカでは、初デートの48%がお別れのキスで締めくくります。

ASK
CAROLINE
... ABOUT SEX

キャロライン姉さんに質問！
セックスについて。

immediately ... すぐに　going steady ... 恋人になる　mature ... 成熟した　can tell right away ... すぐに分かる　pressure ... プレッシャー　teenager ... 10代(13～19歳) rarely ... まれに、めったに～ない　acknowledgment ... 認めること、確認すること　non-existent ... 存在しないこと　society ... 社会　a shame that ... ～は恥である、不名誉である、残念である

セックスについて

素敵だなと思う人と初めて会った日にセックスしますか？

イエスの時もあります。西洋人女性の中には、素敵だと思う人とすぐにセックスする人もいれば、デートを何度かしてからという人もいます。付き合い始めてしばらくしてからという人もいるし、結婚前はダメという人だって、少数派だけどまだいます！年齢にもよるでしょう。若い女性は付き合い始めてすぐにセックスしない傾向がある一方で、成熟した女性は自分をよく知っているので、自分がしたいかどうかすぐに分かるようです。でもいまだに女性には、会ってすぐにはセックスしないものというプレッシャーがあります。

出会ったばかりの人とセックスをすることについて、常によく考えるべきだと思います。また、あなたがどこで誰といるか、他の人に必ず知らせるようにして、必ずコンドームを使うようにしましょう。

SEX

Do you have sex the first time you meet someone you're attracted to?

Sometimes, yes. Some Western women immediately have sex with someone they find attractive, but some have sex with someone after going on a few dates. Some have sex after going steady for a while, and a few still believe in no sex before marriage! It often depends on age, too; younger women tend not to have sex so early in a relationship, whereas more mature women tend to know themselves better and can tell right away if they want to have sex. But women still have quite a lot of pressure not to have sex with someone as soon as they meet them.

You should always be careful when thinking about having sex after you have just met someone; make sure that others know where you are and who you are with, and always use a condom.

セックスについて

キャロラインの場合

10代の女性は、セックスへのすごい圧力をかけられていると思います。そして、間違った理由からセックスすることが多いようです。友達がしているから、彼氏がしたがるから、彼に好かれたいから、愛されていると感じられるから、など。自分の気持ちを考えることはあまりないようです。私は10代には二度と戻りたくないです！

20代前半になっても、女性とセックスには多くのプレッシャーがあると思います。この歳になると、付き合いだしてすぐセックスすることについて、多くの女性が心配するようです。セックスしたがることで、男性が自分への敬意を失うのではないかと感じるからです。これもまた女性の本当の性的な感情とは無関係です。

私は、30代になって初めて、本当に性的に自立していると感じることができるようになりました。同年代の女友達の多くが、同じように感じたようです。相手の男性や友達、社会が自分のことをどう思おうと気にせずに、自分がしたいときにしたい相手とセックスをするのです。ただ、自らの性欲を探索するのに充分な自信が持てる歳になる頃には、多くの女性が結婚し子供を持っていることは残念でなりません。

Caroline's Story

I think that teenage girls are under an awful lot of pressure to have sex and often have sex for the wrong reasons: their friends are doing it, their boyfriend wants them to, they want a guy to like them, or they think it will make them feel loved. Very rarely do they actually think about having sex for their own needs. I would not want to be a teenager again!

Even in our early twenties, I think there is still a lot of pressure around women and sex. At that age, a lot of women worry about having sex too early in a relationship because being too willing to have sex might make the guy lose respect for them. Again, for many women, there is no acknowledgment of one's real sexual feelings.

I found my thirties were the first time for me to feel truly sexually independent. A lot of my girlfriends of the same age felt the same. We would have sex when we wanted and with whom we wanted and really not care about what the man, our friends, or society thought of us. It is a shame that so many women are married with children by the time they have enough confidence to explore their own sexuality.

セックスについて

one-night stand（一晩限りの関係）
Sex with someone for one night only, without the assumption that there will be further sexual encounters. 誰かと、その後も性的な関係が続くという前提なしに一夜限りのセックスをすること。

- "I had a one-night stand last night"
  「昨日の夜、一晩だけの関係を持っちゃった」

- "I don't like one-night stands"
  「ゆきずりの関係は嫌だわ」

- "I think he wanted it to be more than just a one-night stand, but I'm not looking for a relationship at the moment"
  「彼は一晩限りの関係で終わらせたくないみたいだけど、私は今誰ともお付き合いするつもりはないの」

casual sex（カジュアル・セックス）
Sex without special feelings for the other person. 相手に対し特別な感情なくするセックス。

- "I enjoy casual sex because it isn't complicated"
  「カジュアル・セックスが好きなの、複雑な関係にならないから」

- "I'm not into casual sex"
  「私はカジュアル・セックスには興味ないわ」

SEX

one thing led to another（物事が次々と起こって）

Letting things follow a natural course of events; not really stopping anything happening to you. 自分に起こっていることを遮ったりせずに、物事を自然な成り行きに任せること。

- "We were kissing on the sofa and then one thing led to another"
「ソファに座ってキスしていたんだけど、それがどんどん先に進んでっちゃったの」

- "One thing led to another and suddenly we were in bed together"
「いろんなことが重なって、気づいたら一緒にベッドにいたわ」

- "Be careful one thing doesn't lead to another! You know what happens every time you see your ex-boyfriend!"
「次々とコトが起こらないように気をつけてね！あなたが元カレと会うたびに何が起こるか分かってるでしょ！」

to sleep with（〜と寝る） To have sex with. セックスをすること。

- "I slept with one of my colleagues after Friday night's work party, and I hope he'll be OK about it on Monday"
「金曜夜にあった職場の飲み会の後に同僚とエッチしちゃったんだけど、彼、月曜日に気にしてなければいいなぁ」

- "I really want to sleep with him, but I've got my period today!"
「すごく彼と寝たいんだけど、今日生理なのよ！」

- "He wants to sleep with me, but I don't feel ready yet"
「彼はセックスしたがっているんだけど、私はまだ早いと思うの」

セックスについて

TALKING POINTS
トーキング・ポイント

- What do you think about not having sex before marriage?
  結婚前にセックスをしないことに関してどう思いますか？

- How would you handle a situation where you felt pressured to have sex before you were ready?
  心の準備が出来る前にセックスをするプレッシャーがかけられた状況にいたとして、あなただったらどのように対処しますか？

- What do you think are the good and bad elements of a one-night stand?
  行きずりのセックスのいい面、悪い面は何だと思いますか？

- What about the good and bad elements of monogamy?
  浮気をしない関係のいい面、悪い面は？

- What kind of contraception is available in Japan?
  日本でできる避妊法は何ですか？

- Who do you think should have responsibility for ensuring contraception is used?
  避妊をする責任は誰が持つべきだと思いますか？

- Would you know where to go for an STD check-up?
  性感染症の診断はどこへ行けばいいか知っていますか？

Did you know?
45% of Westerners have had a one-night stand.
西洋人女性の45%は一夜限りの関係を持ったことがあります。

ASK
CAROLINE
... ABOUT UNDERWEAR

キャロライン姉さんに質問！
下着について。

sanitary pad ... ナプキン period ... 生理 underwear line ... 下着のライン buttocks ... お尻 lacy ... レースの gusset ... クロッチ部分の布 yeast infection ... イースト菌感染症 to be fascinated by ... 〜に魅了される thrilled ... ドキドキ、ワクワクした状態 to pop to ... ひょいっとどこかへ行く

下着について

**外国の女性はどんな下着をつけるの？
私の同僚のイングランド人は、
パンツの上から下着が出ていることが
あるので分かるんですが、
鮮やかな色のTバックを履いています。
でも私はいっつも大きな木綿の
パンティを履いています。こっちの方が
快適だと思うのですが。**

外国人女性だって、大きな木綿のパンティを履くことはあります！スポーツをする時や生理中にタンポンではなくナプキンを使うときなど特にそうです。確かに、服に下着のラインが出ないのでTバックを履く西洋人女性は多いです。お尻を覆うパンティより、Tバックの方がずっと履きやすいと多くが感じるようです。レースが豊富でセクシーなもの、木綿のシンプルなものなど、色々な色やスタイルのTバックがあります。クロッチ部分の補強布が木綿のTバックは日本であまり見ませんが、木綿でないものはイースト菌感染症になる可能性があるため、外国人女性は木綿の補強布があるものを好みます。

自宅にいるときに髪を束ねるものが見当たらない場合、実はTバックが完璧にその役割を果たしてくれます！外出する際には外すことを忘れないように！

UNDERWEAR

What kind of underwear do non-Japanese women wear? My English colleagues wear brightly coloured thongs that I can sometimes see over the top of their trousers, but I always wear big cotton panties because I think they are more comfortable.

Non-Japanese women wear big cotton panties sometimes, too! Especially for sports or if they use sanitary pads and not tampons when they have their period. But it is true, many of us wear thongs because you don't get underwear lines through your clothes. A lot of women find thongs much more comfortable than panties that cover the buttocks. You can get thongs in lots of different colours and also in different styles—some are lacy and sexy, some are plain cotton thongs. It is quite difficult to find thongs in Japan that have cotton gussets and we prefer to have cotton because non-cotton gussets can cause yeast infections.

If you cannot find anything to tie your hair up with when you are hanging out in your apartment, a thong actually works perfectly! Just remember to take your hair down before going out!

下着について

キャロラインの場合

とある日本人の私の女友達は、私の下着に夢中でした！彼女はいつも私の下着を見たがり、何色でどんなスタイルのものを着けているのか知りたがりました。私はいつもTバックを履いているのですが、彼女は一度も試したことがなく、いつも履き心地がいいか聞いてきました。イングランドに戻った時、人気のある下着店で彼女のためにTバックを1パック買って帰ることにしました。彼女にTバックをあげると、とても喜んでくれました！彼女はさっそくトイレに入り、おニューの下着に着替え、私たちはその晩の予定をそのまま続けました。

私たちは何軒かのバーに行き、結構な量のお酒を飲みました。ところが、しばらく飲んでいるとその友達が私のところに来て、1時間くらい前に突然生理が始まったので、ナプキンを使わなければいけなかった、と私に告げました。そして、そのナプキンを失くしてしまった、と言うんです！おニューのTバックにナプキンを付けるのが上手くいかなかったので、きっとどこかで落として失くしてしまったんです！こんなことが起こったなんて信じられず、今でも私たちの間で笑い話になっています。その友達は、ナプキンを使う時はTバックを使わない、と学びました！

UNDERWEAR

Caroline's Story

My Japanese girlfriend was fascinated by my underwear! She always wanted to look at it and see what colour and style I was wearing. I always wear thongs, which she had never tried, so she was always asking me whether I was comfortable or not. During a trip to England, I decided to buy her a pack of thongs from a very popular underwear store. I gave her the thongs and she was thrilled! She popped to the toilet and changed into her new underwear, and we carried on with our evening.

We went to a few bars and had quite a few drinks. At one point in the evening, my friend came up to me and told me that she had suddenly got her period an hour or so before, so she had used a sanitary pad. Then she told me that she had lost the sanitary pad! She had difficulty getting the sanitary pad to stick to her new thong, and at some point it must have fallen off and disappeared! We couldn't believe this had happened and still laugh about it now! And now she knows not to use a sanitary pad when she is wearing a thong!

下着について

different kinds of underwear
下着の種類

- Tバック: G-string, thong (US), T-back (US) ... Not to be confused with the Australian "thongs," which are a kind of sandal, or with the tea bag! サンダルの一種であるオーストラリアの「ソングス」や、紅茶のティーパックと間違わないようにしてくださいね。

- パンティ: panties (US), pants (UK), knickers (UK) ... Be careful, because American people use "pants" to refer to "trousers," whereas in the UK it means underwear! アメリカ英語でズボンのことを「パンツ」と言いますが、ブリティッシュ英語でパンツは下着を意味しますので気をつけてください！

undies（下着）
Underwear; can mean just panties or both bra and pants, or any other kind of intimate clothing. パンティだけをさす場合もあれば、パンティとブラの両方をさす場合もあります。

- "I received some sexy new undies for my birthday!"
  「誕生日にセクシーな下着をもらったの！」

- "I always feel sexy when I'm wearing matching undies!"
  「上下お揃いの下着を着ているといつもセクシーな気分になるわ！」

UNDERWEAR

granny pants（おばあちゃんパンツ） Big knickers that cover your whole bottom (also known as "Bridget Jones" pants after the scene where she goes on a date with Hugh Grant's character wearing big knickers). お尻全体を包み込む巨大なパンツ（またの名を「ブリジット・ジョーンズ」パンツ。これは、ヒュー・グラント演じる登場人物とのデートのシーンでブリジットが巨大なパンツを履いていたからです）。

- "I haven't done any laundry for ages—all I've got left now are lots of granny pants!"
  「ずいぶん長いこと洗濯していないから、おばあちゃんパンツしか残ってないわ！」

- "I'm throwing out all my granny pants and replacing them with some sexy new underwear!"
  「おばあちゃんパンツは全部捨てて、セクシーな下着を新調するわ！」

- "G-strings are so uncomfortable! I'll take my granny pants any day!"
  「Tバックって超履きづらい！おばあちゃんパンツの方がよっぽどいいわ！」

going commando（ノーパンになる） Not wearing any underwear. パンティを履かないこと。

- "I've got a dress that is so tight, the only way I can wear it is by going commando!"
  「ものすごくキツいドレスを持っているんだけど、キツすぎてノーパンにならないと着られないの！」

- "I always go commando when I sleep—I don't think it's healthy to keep it all covered up!"
  「寝る時はいつもノーパンよ。常に覆っているなんて不健康だわ！」

- "I've always wanted to go commando, but I'm too nervous!"
  「ノーパンで過ごしてみたいっていつも思うんだけど、緊張しちゃうの！」

下着について

TALKING POINTS
トーキング・ポイント

- What is your favourite kind of underwear and why?
  あなたのお気に入りの下着は何ですか？それはなぜですか？

- How about your favourite underwear shop in Japan?
  日本で好きな下着ショップはどこですか？

- Getting your first bra is a big deal for many English girls. Do you remember getting your first bra?
  多くのイングランド人女性にとって、初めてブラを買うことは大きな出来事です。初めてブラを買った時のことを覚えていますか？

- Do you have different kinds of underwear for different occasions?
  状況に応じて使い分ける、種類の違う下着を持っていますか？

- Do you have special underwear that is just for dates?
  デート専用の勝負下着を持っていますか？

- Have you ever tried going without underwear?
  下着を着けないで出かけたことはありますか？

- What do you think about the vending machines in Japan that sell used underwear?
  使用済みの下着を売る自動販売機が日本にあることについて、どう思いますか？

Did you know?
The satin thong worn by Christina Aguilera for a cover shoot for *Maxim Magazine* was sold on eBay for about ¥175,000.
クリスティーナ・アギレラが雑誌『マキシム』の表紙を飾った際に付けていた絹のTバックがeBayで約175,000円で売却されました。

ASK
CAROLINE
... ABOUT CAREERS

キャロライン姉さんに質問!
キャリアについて。

to quit work ... 仕事を辞める to afford to ... 〜する余裕がある bored ... 退屈した to waste ... 無駄にする prospective ... 見込みのある、将来の expectation ... 期待、予想 to request ... 要請する flexibility ... 柔軟性のあること if only ... もし〜さえしたら decision ... 決意

キャリアについて

日本人女性は、結婚すると仕事を辞める人が多く、ほとんどの場合、喜んでそうしています。西洋人の女性は、結婚すると仕事を辞めますか？

ほとんどの西洋人女性は、多くの理由から結婚後に仕事を辞めることはありません。ほとんどの夫婦が1人の給料では生活できないので、いずれにせよ共働きをする必要があるでしょう。ほとんどの女性が、世話をする子供もいないうちに仕事を辞めたら時間を持て余すので、仕事を続けたいと思うのです。また、キャリアを築くために一生懸命働いてきた女性は、仕事を辞めれば努力が水の泡になる、と感じるでしょう。一般的に、西洋人は結婚したという理由だけで女性が仕事を辞めるものだとは考えていません。

日本の企業は時に、女性スタッフは結婚したら会社を辞めるものだと思うようです。将来雇用者となり得る会社とは、相手側が何を期待しているのかきちんと話し合うことが大切です。もしあなたが、今後しばらく結婚するつもりはないとしてもですよ！

CAREERS

Many Japanese women quit their jobs after marriage and, for the most part, they are happy to do this. Do Western women quit their jobs after marriage?

Most Western women do not quit work after marriage for many reasons. Most couples could not afford to live on just one person's salary, so both of them have to work anyway. Most women would probably be bored if they gave up their job and did not have children to take care of, so they want to continue working. And women who had worked very hard to build a career would feel all that hard work would have been wasted if they gave up work. In general, Westerners do not expect a woman to give up work just because she has got married.

Sometimes Japanese companies expect female staff to quit after marriage. It is important to talk to a prospective employer about their expectations even if you don't plan on getting married for a long time!

キャリアについて

キャロラインの場合

結婚をして仕事を辞めたという西洋人女性を私は一人も知りません。でも、赤ちゃんが出来たから仕事を辞めざるを得なかった、という西洋人女性を何人か知っています。大学を主席で卒業した友達は、素晴らしい仕事を得て、その仕事を心から楽しんでいました。30代前半で結婚し、その後すぐに妊娠しました。

彼女は雇用主から出産休暇をもらい、仕事に復帰できるようになった際、勤務時間を多少フレキシブルにして欲しいと願い出ました。ダブルインカムなので、託児所を使うことも出来たのですが(英国では託児所は日本よりもかなり高くなります)、何か起こった時のために、フレキシブルでいたいと思ったのです。会社は、彼女がフレックス・タイムで働くことを許さなかったので、仕事を辞めざるを得ませんでした。一人の給与では託児所に払うお金を賄うことができなかったので、赤ちゃんの面倒をみるために彼女は家にいるという、まったく計画していなかった状態になっています。

多くの西洋人女性は、結婚ばかりか出産後でも仕事を辞めるなんて考えません。こうした女性の決意を、より多くの企業が支援してくれたら、ハッピーなお母さんがもっと増えるのに!と思います。

CAREERS

Caroline's Story

I don't know any Western women who have quit work after they have got married. But I do know a few Western women who have had to quit work after having a baby. My friend was a top student at university. She got an extremely good job, which she loved. She got married in her early thirties, and got pregnant quite soon after.

Her employer gave her maternity leave, and when she was able to return to work, she requested a little bit of flexibility in her hours. With two incomes, they could afford day care (which is much more expensive in the UK than it is in Japan), but she wanted to have a little bit of flexibility in case something happened. Her company wouldn't allow her to have a flexible schedule, so she had to quit her job. They couldn't afford day care on just one salary, so now she has to stay at home taking care of the baby, which isn't what she had planned to do at all.

Many Western women would not expect to quit work after marriage, nor would they expect to after childbirth. If only more companies could support that decision, I am sure we would have a lot of happier mothers!

キャリアについて

DINK … Double Income, No Kids（ディンクス…共働きで子供のない夫婦）
Both partners in a couple are earning a good salary and spend it on themselves because they choose not to have children. 夫婦が共に良い給料を稼いでおり、子供を作らないことを選んで代わりに自分たちのためにお金を使います。

- "They live in a DINK household"
  「彼らはディンクスの家に住んでいるんだ」

- "My employer wants us to start targeting the DINK market"
  「雇用主がディンクスの市場をターゲットにしろって言ってる」

house-husband（主夫）
Male partner who assumes domestic responsibilities while the other partner works in paid employment. カップルのうち男性の方が家事を行い、もう1人が外に働きに出ます。結婚していない場合やゲイのカップルでも使えます。

- "After the baby comes, I will go back to work and my partner will be a house-husband"
  「赤ちゃんが生まれたら、私は仕事に戻って主人が主夫をやるの」

- "I'm looking for a potential house-husband right now!"
  「主夫になってくれる人を探しています！」

CAREERS

equal opportunities employer (機会均等な雇用主)
Employer who treats people the same, regardless of gender, age, marital status, race, or sexuality. 性別、年齢、配偶者の有無、人種、性的志向に関わりなく誰をも平等に扱う雇用主。

- "My boss would never expect me to leave work just because I got married—the company is genuinely an equal opportunities employer"
  「私の上司は、私が結婚したからといって私が会社を辞めるとは思っていないわ。うちの会社って、本当に機会均等な雇用主なの」

- "I'm tired of being treated differently in my company just because I am a woman ... It's time to find an equal opportunities employer!"
  「女性だからってだけで会社で他の人と違うように扱われるのにもう飽き飽き。機会均等な雇用主を探す時かも」

- "My company is trying to become a more equal opportunities employer"
  「うちの会社は、より機会均等な雇用主になろうとしています」

to make a living (生計を立てる)
To work; to earn money. 働くこと、お金を稼ぐこと。

- "We both have to make a living if we want nice vacations together"
  「一緒に素敵なところに旅行に行きたいなら、お互いお金を稼がなきゃいけないわよ」

- "I like to make my own living; I don't want to depend on my husband"
  「自分で自分の生計は立てたいの。夫に頼りたくはないわ」

- "I love what I do to make a living! I wouldn't give it up if I got married!"
  「自分の仕事がすごく好きなの！結婚したって辞めないわよ」

キャリアについて

TALKING POINTS
トーキング・ポイント

- How do you feel about your job?
  あなたは自分の仕事についてどう思いますか？

- What do you think about quitting work after marriage?
  結婚して仕事を辞めることについてどう思いますか？

- If you quit your job after getting married, how did this affect your life?
  もし結婚して退職した経験がある場合、それがあなたの人生にどう影響しましたか？

- If you stayed, how did your colleagues react?
  もし仕事を辞めなかった場合、同僚の反応はどうでしたか？

- Do you think some companies are more supportive than others of married women who work? How so?
  既婚の働く女性に対し、他の会社と比べ協力的な会社があると思いますか？どうしてですか？

- Do you think that marriage can affect a woman's career in a good way or a bad way? How about a man's career?
  女性のキャリアの中で、結婚はいい影響があると思いますか？悪い影響があると思いますか？男性のキャリアではどうでしょうか？

Did you know?
Research has shown that 85% of women who are offered flexible working arrangements accept them.
とある調査によると、フレキシブルな勤務時間をオファーされた女性の85%が、それを受け入れています。

ASK
CAROLINE
... ABOUT MOTHERHOOD

キャロライン姉さんに質問！
母親として。

to sacrifice ... 犠牲にする needs ... 要求、ニーズ to see themselves ... 自認する to revolve around ... ～を中心に展開する to maintain a balance ... バランスを維持する aspect ... 側面 conscious effort ... 意図的な努力 flexible ... 柔軟性のある、融通の利く to make a point of ... 努めて～する occasionally ... 折りに触れ to fulfill ... 満たす role model ... ロール・モデル、模範になる人

母親として

> 西洋人女性はどうして、子供が出来た後でさえ社交的な活動を続け、自立し続けるのですか？日本人は、子供のために自分を犠牲にするのは美しいと思う傾向があります。

西洋の文化では、子供のために自分を犠牲にするという考えは少し古臭かったりします。私たちの母親世代はそういう人が多かったでしょうが、その頃は選択肢があまりなかったのです。西洋人女性の多くは、赤ちゃんができたからといって自分の人生を生きることを止める必要はないと考えます。自分たちを、母親としてだけでなく、ニーズを持った個人として見ているのです。私たちは、配偶者や友達と社交的でいることは大切だと思っています。多くが、親の人生が自分たち中心だと思いつつ子供が成長するのは不健康だと信じています。

子供を持たない友達を持ち続けることは、社交的な生活とのバランスを維持するのに素晴らしい方法です——彼女たちは、あなたに子供が出来たからというだけで誘わなくなるなんてことはしませんから！

MOTHERHOOD

Why do Western women try to continue their social lives and to be independent even after they have a baby? Japanese tend to think that sacrificing your own needs for your children is a beautiful idea.

The idea of sacrificing yourself for your children is a little bit old-fashioned in Western culture. Many of our mothers did that, but they didn't have a lot of choice. Many Western women believe that their own lives should not stop just because they have a baby. They see themselves as not just being a mother, but also a person with her own needs. We think it is important to have a social life with our partners and with our friends. Many believe that it is not healthy for children to grow up believing that their parents' lives revolve around them.

Keeping friends who do not have children is a great way to maintain a balance in your social life. After all, they won't stop inviting you out just because you have kids!

母親として

キャロラインの場合

私には日本人男性と結婚しているオーストラリア人の女友達がいて、2人には小さい娘がいます。結婚前の彼女はとても自立していて、旦那さんもそれを知っていました。彼女は結婚時や出産時、自分の人生をある程度は喜んで変えるつもりでしたが、自立し続けることは彼女にとってとても重要なことでした。妊娠した時に仕事を辞めたのですが、授乳が終わるくらいに赤ちゃんが大きくなると、すぐにパートタイムの仕事を見つけました。そして子供がいない男友達や女友達を探そうと意識的に努力したのでした。

その結果、彼女はバランスの取れた生活スタイルを作り出しました。仕事がパートタイムなので、子供の具合が悪くなり自宅に戻る必要がある時に柔軟に対応できます。さらに、独身の友達や子供のいない友達からのお誘いは必ず受けるようにしています。時に旦那さん、たまに子供を連れてくることもありますが、ほとんどの場合は彼女1人で参加します。大変ですが、彼女は妻や母としての責任を果たすと同時に、個人としての欲求も満たしています。

彼女の女友達や女性の同僚は彼女を素敵な手本とみており、彼女の娘もきっと将来彼女を見習うだろうと私は確信しています。

MOTHERHOOD

Caroline's Story

My Australian girlfriend is married to a Japanese man and they have a young daughter. She was a very independent person before she got married, and her husband knew this. She was happy to change some aspects of her life when she got married and had a baby, but maintaining her independence was important to her. She stopped working when she got pregnant, but as soon as her baby was old enough to stop breast-feeding, she found a part-time job, and she also made a conscious effort to seek out male and female friends who did not have children.

She has created a very balanced lifestyle for herself; her part-time job allows her flexible hours in case her baby gets sick and she has to go home. And she makes a point of accepting invitations from her single friends or friends without children. Sometimes she brings her husband, and occasionally her child, but mostly she goes alone. While it is a challenge, she manages to fulfill her responsibilities as a wife and mother, but also her needs as an individual.

Her female friends and colleagues consider her to be a great role model and I know her daughter will see her as a great role model, too.

母親として

sacrifice（犠牲にする） Giving something up for something considered to have a higher value. より高い価値があると思われるもののために、何かを諦めること。

- "My mum sacrificed her career to have children"
  「私の母は、子供を持つためにキャリアを犠牲にしました」

- "There are some great day care services available, so I can maintain a balance and not sacrifice either my career or my children!"
  「素晴らしい託児所があるので、仕事と子供を犠牲にすることなくバランスを保てるの！」

old-fashioned（古臭い） Outdated. 時代遅れ。

- "I think giving up work after marriage is rather old-fashioned"
  「結婚したから仕事を辞めるなんて、ちょっと古臭いと思うわ」

- "It's a little bit old-fashioned nowadays to assume that a woman would change her name after marriage"
  「結婚したからって女性が苗字を変えると決めるつけるなんて、最近ではちょっと古臭いわよ」

MOTHERHOOD

independent（自立している、主体性がある）Not relying on anybody else except yourself. 自分以外の誰にも頼らないでいること。

- "I like to be financially independent, so my husband and I have separate bank accounts and split everything equally"
  「金銭的に自立していたいから、夫と別の銀行口座を持ってすべてを平等に分けているの」

- "We've been going steady for a year, but I'm still not ready to move in with him—I value my independence too much"
  「付き合って1年になるけど、まだ彼と一緒に住む気になれないの。自立していることって大切だと思うから」

- "One of the difficult things about deciding to have a baby is working out whether I am ready to give up my independence yet"
  「子供を生むって決めるのが難しい理由の1つに、私が自立を諦められるかどうか考えなきゃいけないってことがあるわ」

role model（お手本、ロール・モデル）Someone that others, especially younger people, look up to and are influenced by. 他の人、特に若い人が尊敬し、影響を受ける人。

- "I try to be a positive role model for my daughter"
  「娘にとって前向きなお手本でありたいと思っているの」

- "My mum was such a great role model for me as I grew up"
  「私が大人になっていく過程で、母は素晴らしいロール・モデルだったわ」

母親として

TALKING POINTS
トーキング・ポイント

- Did you see your mother trying to keep some independence when you were a child?
  あなたが子供だった頃、あなたのお母さんは自立しようとしていたと思いますか?

- If you have children, do you try to meet your own needs as well as theirs?
  もしあなたに子供がいる場合、子供のニーズ同様、自分のニーズも満たそうとしますか?

- How do you think mothers could take care of themselves as well as their children?
  母親が、子供の面倒を見るのと同様に自分の面倒も見ることができることについてどう思いますか?

- What kind of role do you think fathers could play in supporting mothers' independence? And how could the extended family support this?
  母親の主体性を支援するために、父親が出来る役目は何だと思いますか?また、近親者はどのようにこれを支援できると思いますか?

- Do you think there are any negative aspects to mothers who try to maintain their independence?
  自立性を維持しようとする母親について、なにかマイナス面はあると思いますか?

Did you know?
Of the one in three babies born in the United States to unwed mothers, 60% are born to women older than 30.
アメリカでは赤ちゃんの3人に1人が未婚の母の元に生まれ、そうした未婚の母の60%は30歳以上の女性です。

ASK CAROLINE
... ABOUT BEAUTY

キャロライン姉さんに質問!
美について。

difference ... 違い youth ... 若さ to sexualize ... 性的に扱う、性的な対象とする to portray as ... 〜として描く experienced ... 経験豊富な feminism ... フェミニズム potential ... 可能性のある confused ... 混乱した unattractive ... 魅力のない to experiment ... 試す、実験する to question ... 問いかける、疑問に思う to achieve ... 至る、達成する to pamper ... 甘やかす

美について

日本人女性はかわいくなりたいと思うものですが、外国人女性はどうしてセクシーでいたいと思うのですか？

セクシーか、かわいいかの違いではありません。日本ではかわいいことがセクシーとされます。違いは、女性らしいか、子供らしいかです。外国人女性は一般的に、年齢を問わず成熟した女性と見られたいので、そう振る舞います。日本人女性は年齢を問わず若い女性と見られたいので、そう振る舞います。日本では若さが性的に扱われる傾向があります。日本では女子高生がセクシーとされ、一方で西洋文化では成熟し経験豊かで自信のある女性がセクシーとされます。「cute」は子供や小動物を表すのによく使われるので、西洋人女性はかわいいなんて思われたくないんです！

外側の「かわいらしさ」より、内側の自信をもっと磨くことに焦点を当てれば、あなたの外側も内側も、すべての面を分かってくれる、しかるべき友達やパートナーをもっと惹き付けることが出来ることでしょう。

BEAUTY

Why do foreign women want to be sexy, whereas Japanese women want to be cute?

The difference is not about being sexy or cute. In Japan, being cute is considered sexy. The difference is about being woman-like or child-like. Foreign women generally like to look and behave like mature women, whatever their age. Japanese women tend to like to look and behave like young women, whatever their age. In Japan, youth tends to be sexualized. High school girls are portrayed as sexy, whereas in Western culture, mature, experienced, and confident women tend to be considered sexy. Cute tends to be used to describe children or small animals, and a Western woman wouldn't want to be considered cute!

If you focus on developing your inner confidence rather than your outer "cuteness," you will attract more appropriate friends and partners who will appreciate all aspects of you, both inside and out!

美について

キャロラインの場合

私はとても強い母親に育てられ、大学ではフェミニズムを勉強しました。私は常に、内側の美しさを育てるよう、そして友達や将来のパートナーから見たら私の自信や人生経験が私をより魅力的にすると考えるよう励まされました。なので、外見なんてあまり興味がありませんでした。メイクもあまりしなかったし、お肌のお手入れもどうすればいいか分からないし興味もなかったんです！

来日したばかりの頃、セクシーとは何なのかよく分からなくなってしまいました。なぜそんなに若く見られたいのかや、外見に気をかけすぎることがなぜいいとされているのか、理解できなかったんです。自分が魅力のない女性に思えてきて、すっかり自信をなくしてしまいました。色んなファッションスタイルやメイクも試し、自分の内側の強さは一体魅力的なのか、なんて疑問に思ったりもしました！

日本に来て数年が過ぎ、内面と外見の美に対する考え方について、私が思う健全なバランスに辿り着きました。今はメイクを楽しんでいるし、お手入れに時間をかけることも大好きです。それでも、私の内面が常に一番大切であるということも分かっています。

BEAUTY

Caroline's Story

I was brought up by a very strong mother and studied feminism at university. I had always been encouraged to develop my inner beauty and to see confidence and life experience as the things that would make me attractive to friends and potential partners. I wasn't very interested in how I looked on the outside. I didn't wear much make-up and had no idea or interest in how to take care of my skin!

When I first came to Japan, I was very confused about what seemed to be considered sexy. I couldn't understand why wanting to look so young and paying so much attention to one's looks was considered to be a good thing. I started to feel unattractive and lost a lot of confidence. I experimented with a lot of different clothing styles and make-up, and questioned whether my inner strength was attractive at all!

After my first few years in Japan, I achieved what I consider to be a healthy balance in my attitude toward my inner and outer beauty. I enjoy wearing make-up now and enjoy spending time pampering myself, but I know that what is inside me is really what matters.

美について

Synonyms for cute（「cute」の同意語）

- adorable … 愛らしい
- delightful … 愛嬌のある
- charming … チャーミング
- endearing … かわいらしい
- sweet … かわいい

Synonyms for sexy（「sexy」の同意語）

- hot … 刺激的な
- arousing … 刺激的な
- sensual … 官能的な
- seductive … 誘惑的な
- desirable … 性的魅力のある

BEAUTY

Alternatives（他の言い方）

- Instead of "I think she is cute," use "I think she is attractive"
「彼女ってかわいいと思う」の代わりに、「彼女って魅力的だと思う」と表現しましょう。

- Instead of "That's a cute blouse," use "That's a pretty blouse"
「かわいいブラウスね」の代わりに、「可憐なブラウスね」と表現しましょう。

- Instead of "Your make-up is cute," use "Your make-up is striking/cool/sexy"
「かわいいメイクね」の代わりに、「印象的な／カッコイイ／セクシーなメイクね」と表現しましょう。

- Instead of "You always look cute," use "You always look stylish"
「あなたっていつもかわいいわね」の代わりに「あなたっていつもおしゃれね」と表現しましょう。

Usage（使い方）

- Cute usage: puppies, kittens, babies, toddlers, small children's clothes
「かわいい」を使うのは：子犬、子猫、赤ちゃん、幼児、子供服

- Sexy usage: adult women, adult women's clothes, make-up
「セクシー」を使うのは：大人の女性、大人の女性の服、メイク

79

美について

TALKING POINTS
トーキング・ポイント

- What do you think makes a woman look sexy, stylish, and confident?
  あなたは、女性をセクシーでおしゃれで自信を持っているように見せるのは何だと思いますか？

- When do you feel at your strongest and most confident?
  あなたがもっとも強く、自信を感じるのはどんな時ですか？

- How do you feel about growing older?
  歳を重ねることに対してどう感じますか？

- How much value do you put on your own appearance?
  あなたは自分の外見にどのくらいの価値を置きますか？

- And the appearance of others?
  他人の外見はどうでしょうか？

- How do you think society portrays women as they grow older?
  女性が年を取ると、社会は女性をどのように描写すると思いますか？

- What cultural differences do you see in how older women are treated?
  年を取った女性がどう扱われるかについて、どんな文化的違いがあると思いますか？

Did you know?
Asian people place more value on looks rather than personality than any other group. 34% of Asian people say that looks are more important.
アジア人は他のグループと比べ、性格よりも外見により価値を置きます。アジア人の34％が、外見がより重要であるとしています。

2010
Alexandra Press
Also available for the iPad and iPhone.

Check out the student's edition of the first in the *Ask Caroline* series for Japanese women and their foreign female private language teachers. For bulk orders or enquiries from language schools, contact info@carolinepover.com.

Coming soon! The second in the *Ask Caroline* series contains the following topics:
- Priorities when choosing a job.
- Working with or for men.
- Which is more important, work or marriage?
- Do Western women find Japanese men attractive?
- Hugging your friends.
- Boobs and their shapes and sizes.
- Pubic hair removal.
- Childbirth pain relief.
- Karaoke styles.
- Brand name goods.

ISBN 978-4-9900791-8-5　C5882　¥952E

2002
Alexandra Press

Tokyo Pub Crawler

his & her bar guide
dan riney & gia payne

Take a regular, beer-loving guy and a prissy, outlandish coquette; give them a pen, some paper, and hours upon hours to visit most of the bars worth seeing in Tokyo, and you have ... **Tokyo Pub Crawler** ... an honest and irreverent collection of critiques on some of the most popular and well-hidden watering holes in the city. Get both points of view: the guy's lowdown and the girl's dish.

Full of bar-hopper-friendly features, including happy hour times, maps that lead you from the station to the barstool, last train times for the Yamanote line, cover and table charges, a rating system even a drunk can understand, what to wear, and who you'll meet.

And it's thankfully devoid of irritating rubbish like useless, misleading doublespeak; sneaky bar advertorials; and reviews for places that demand fluent Japanese.

ISBN 4-99007911-6   C2065   ¥952E

2006
Alexandra Press

Tokyo English Life Line has served the international community for over 36 years, and some of their wealth of accumulated knowledge and information is available, packed into this pocket-sized resource.

TELL me about Tokyo is a vital companion in any situation, placing invaluable resources and services at your fingertips. The 12 chapters of this essential handbook and directory cover legal, medical, and religious services, as well as resources for employment, daily living, and more. Whether you are new to Tokyo, or a more seasoned expatriate, this valuable handbook and directory is a resource for everything you need to know about life in this city.

Sponsored by:
PRICEWATERHOUSECOOPERS
Premier WORLDWIDE MOVERS
T 管理職紹介
M 人事労務管理
T 人材育成/自己啓発

TELL contacts
Life Line: 03-5774-0992
URL: http://www.telljp.com

ISBN 4-9900791-5-9   C0026   ¥952E

2007
Alexandra Press

Tokyo: Here and How
An expat's guide to finding your path in the city and beyond...
By Tokyo American Club Women's Group

You're in Tokyo, a city that has everything to offer ... if only you could figure out what's being offered. You want to make the most of it, but don't know how to start chipping away at the madness.

Whether you've been here for five days or five years, **Tokyo: Here and How** is your comforting companion; it will take you from confusion to inspiration, from frustration to fulfillment. This comprehensive guide to life in Tokyo is filled with relevant details that only an experienced expatriate would know.

With reference pullouts, user-friendly maps, and city secrets, **Tokyo: Here and How** will help you navigate the city, avoid confusion, and guide you through emergency situations.

A comprehensive resource, an invaluable companion, and a comforting hand to hold, **Tokyo: Here and How** is your guide to a rewarding time in Tokyo.

ISBN 978-4-9900-7916-1   C0026   ¥4667E

2009
Alexandra Press

GUIDE TO INTERNATIONAL SCHOOLS IN JAPAN

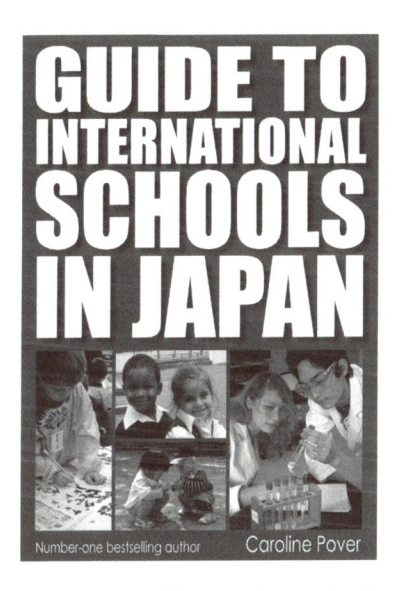

Number-one bestselling author Caroline Pover

"Offers the most in-depth account of Japanese international schools available."
— American father living in Japan

This 700-page guide is essential reading for expatriate parents, internationally-minded Japanese couples, and bicultural families. The first-ever comprehensive guidebook to international schools in Japan, it gives parents the ability to examine over one hundred schools, all in one publication.

This book is also a vital resource for adventurous teachers looking for the perfect school in which to continue their careers.

Based on over 60 questions that parents ask when looking at educational options for their children, this guide is like having a 6-page, 2,000-word mini-prospectus for each of over one hundred schools, all in one handy package!

ISBN 978-4-9900-70-17-8 C0026 ¥4726E (Japanese edition also available)

2001
Alexandra Press

Being A Broad in Japan

Everything a Western woman needs to survive and thrive

Caroline Pover

"My encyclopedia, my translator, my phone book, my best friend!"
—Western woman living in Japan

Now in its fifth printing, **Being A Broad in Japan** includes everything you need to make the most of your life: case studies of Western women working in almost 50 different types of jobs; anecdotes from many of the 200 Western women interviewed; profiles of 23 women's organizations; essential Japanese words and phrases; and indispensable resource sections.

Read about: coping with culture shock, finding clothes and shoes that fit, avoiding hair disasters, cooking Japanese food, telling a *chikan* where to go, dating and the singles scene, organizing contraception, getting married and divorced, adopting a baby, educating your child, finding a job, teaching gender studies in the English-language classroom, and coping with reverse culture shock when you leave Japan.

ISBN 4-9900791-0-8   C5026   ¥2858E

1997~
Being A Broad magazine

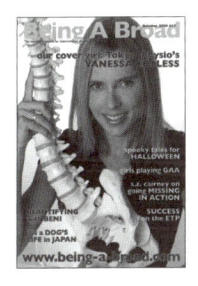

This 28-page monthly magazine features REAL foreign women on the cover (you won't find any airbrushed models here!), and covers a wide range of topics such as health and fitness, clothes and style, professional profiles, employment issues, motherhood, politics, travel, and love!

We feature our favourite new discoveries that help us with life in Japan, and profile women's organizations that contribute to our lives here. We also keep an eye on what's going on elsewhere with our Women of the World page, and have several regular columnists who often have us in fits of laughter! We always welcome new writers, so get in touch to get in print.

If you can't find what you need in the magazine, or have an emergency question to ask, then check out our extremely active discussion board—you'll find a whole host of foreign women ready to help you settle into your life in Japan.

http://www.being-a-broad.com

Caroline Pover arrived in Japan from the United Kingdom in 1996, seeking adventure! Teaching by day, Caroline launched *Being A Broad* magazine for international women in Japan, and wrote and published a book with the same title. She is also the author of the *Guide to International Schools in Japan*, and was a popular columnist for the *Shukan ST* for two years.

Caroline has been recognized for her many contributions to the international women's community, and was awarded Best Entrepreneur by the British Chamber of Commerce in Japan in 2008.

Caroline is passionate about and committed to helping women make the most of their lives, professionally and personally. She lives in Tokyo and can be contacted at caroline@carolinepover.com.

Satomi Matsumaru is a freelance translator who spent six years in the United Kingdom, initially as a student and later as an expatriate writer. She has many years of experience translating in multinational/multilingual environments, covering areas such as entertainment, business, the automotive industry, and finance.

Thanks to her time abroad, and working in cross-cultural environments in both Japan and the United Kingdom, Satomi not only understands the technicalities of her two languages, but also the cultural implications behind them, which makes her translation so much more relevant and meaningful.

Satomi lives in Japan with a fresh love for her native country after all those years abroad, and can be contacted at satomi@carolinepover.com.

http://www.askcaroline.com